How to Make Work Not Suck

CARINA MAGGAR

How to Make Work Not Suck

HONEST ADVICE FOR PEOPLE WITH JOBS

What Am I Doing With My Life?

This is not a self-help book. If it was, I wouldn't be writing this in my pyjamas at 3pm on a Tuesday. I'm not even sure if I would describe it as a career guide.

When I think of guides, I think of travel maps, ones that lead you to a specific destination. I'm definitely not qualified to tell you what the next best move is. If I knew that, I'd be the CEO of a global brand and, once again, I wouldn't be writing this in my pyjamas at 3pm.

I've had many jobs in the past ten years: from selling bath bombs and real estate, to walking dogs, writing blogs, working at a film studio, doing voiceovers and presenting shows online and on TV. I haven't followed any linear pattern; my career decisions have been based on a) desperation b) spontaneity and c) intrigue. Because of my experience as a career butterfly, I have met a lot of people; some are featured throughout this book. I have gathered knowledge from different industries, environments and roles. I've spent time with people from all areas of life, at all stages of their careers, giving me the opportunity to understand, learn and observe how they do what they do.

There are numerous unspoken rules that exist in the world of work. I've considerately shared them in this book, so

you don't have to go through the trouble I have. Just know, I have suffered for you. I can write about making mistakes, failing, blagging, bullshitting, saying the wrong things, doing the wrong things, because I've been there. I'm guilty of practically everything within these pages. Head held high, I can admit I've embarrassed myself a lot, I've got myself into some humiliating situations and I've made questionable decisions. On the other hand, I've surprised and impressed myself too.

What you hold in your hands (even though it's beautiful) is a product of angst, smothered in the uncertainty and confusion of my twenties. This book will provide you with the insights that I wish I'd had at the start of my career, but make no mistake, they never stop being helpful, no matter what stage you're at in life. Whether you're 18 or 40, I guarantee you'll find this book helpful. If you're 18, you'll learn some things you don't know yet. If you're 40, you might be reminded of the things you've forgotten.

And, let's be honest, no one needs another career book written by a middle-aged man.

No One Knows What They're Doing. Neither Should You.

They're all pretending: your boss, first-time parents, the Prime Minister. Everyone's making it up as they go along. You don't have to have all the answers to do a good job. If you're suffering from imposter syndrome or feel out of your depth, know you're not the only one crying in the loo at lunchtime. It's really just a case of who's putting on the best performance.

You Will Have Regrets.

A few years ago, when I was a presenter, I was invited to audition in front of the executive board of directors of a famous TV channel. It was a life-changing opportunity. I'd been asked to deliver a monologue about a celebrity story in the news at the time. Whether it was an extreme case of nerves or a spell of severe delusion, I decided not to prepare (mistake number 1).

I took my seat at the unnecessarily large boardroom table occupied by stern faces in suits, impatiently glancing at their watches. When it was my time to shine, I got up from my chair, sauntered over to the camera, stood on the marked spot, stared down the camera lens and completely froze. I couldn't formulate a thought, let alone a sentence. I speedily moonwalked (mistake number 2) out of the room, apologizing profusely for wasting their time.

We're told not to have regrets, but I have a bucketful. If you learn from them (which I did), they can actually be useful experiences.

THE ART OF CREATIVE BULLSHITTING.

THERE ARE THREE TYPES OF PEOPLE IN THE WORLD:

THOSE WHO BULLSHIT

THOSE WHO BELIEVE OTHER PEOPLE'S BULLSHIT

THOSE WHO BELIEVE THEIR OWN BULLSHIT

AIM TO BE HERE

Everyone's Creative, Even You.

Did you grab a bunch of ingredients from the fridge and cook dinner last night? Did you dress yourself this morning? Do you have to solve complex issues on a weekly basis? That's all creativity; it's problem-solving.

Creativity doesn't need to be placed on a pedestal, it's not an unobtainable thing. We seem to consider creative types as the lucky ones who've been anointed with a sterling silver paintbrush, but creativity isn't mysterious or magical. There's no secret formula or Da Vinci Code to crack.

If you're feeling particularly uncreative, switch up your environment. A lack of inspiration is external, not internal.

There's Nothing Wrong With Wanting to Make Money.

We all know that money brings freedom and security, exotic holidays, fancy dinners, a beautiful home. However, if your ambition is only to make money, then you will always be chasing it, even when there are multiple zeros at the end of your bank balance.

Happiness should be your priority, and you can't buy it in Selfridges. If you're not happy within yourself, you'll remain that way whether you're in a Lamborghini or a Fiat 500. You can't heal an open wound with a £50 note.

The World Is Full of Assholes.

Approximately 8 percent* of people in every office are assholes, unpleasant characters with giant chips on their shoulders. You'll dislike everything about them, from the things they say to the way they walk. If it's any consolation, this will prepare you for life. Because life is also full of assholes. The challenge is not to become one.

The average meeting consists of 7.5 people. Next time you're in the room, take a look around for the one guaranteed asshole.

*THIS IS A MADE-UP STATISTIC, BUT FROM PAST EXPERIENCE, I'M SURE IT'S PRETTY ACCURATE.

Flirt.

Discovering what you want to do is
a process of trial and error. Don't wait
to fall head over heels in love with
a career. If we all actually waited to
marry someone who was patient,
beautiful, hilarious, loyal, a great cook
and a fabulous dancer with brilliant
white teeth, we'd all die single.

A Fat Lie.

Here's a home truth that might sting a little: many of us were raised by our parents to believe we could be anything we wanted. That anything we set our minds to is achievable. Unfortunately, the real world is tough and unpredictable. Sometimes working hard isn't enough. Opportunities don't come knocking at your door, you have to go out and find them.

When you're raised to believe you're destined for success and the world is your oyster, of course you're going to feel like you've failed when things don't turn out the way you'd expected. Have a little self-compassion.

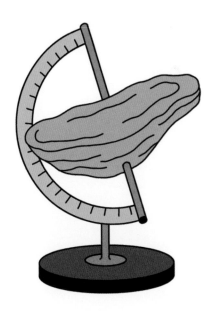

The Office A-Z.

A is for **annual leave**

You're getting paid
to go away, make sure
you do just that.

B is for **bonus**

Something you might get after
your first year, if you're lucky.

C is for **conference calls**

Mostly a total waste
of your time.

D is for **discrimination**

Something you might experience.
If so, see letter **H**.

E is for **equal pay**

Your gender or ethnicity
should not influence
your salary.

F is for **getting fired**

If this happens, say 'thank you'
and exit gracefully.

L is for **losing
the will to live**

This might occur on
a weekly basis.

K is for **knowing your rights**

Be aware of your rights
as an employee. Always
read the contract.

J is for **work jargon**

Try all you like but
you'll soon become
an office parrot.

I is for **interns**

Be nice to them.

H is for **HR**

Go to them with any work-related
personal issues. Ironically, those in
HR can sometimes be unpleasant.

G is for **gossip**

Keep it to yourself.

M is for **management**

Get on their good side. Your life will be easier if they like you.

N is for **notice period**

Usually an awkward month, sometimes longer.

O is for **opportunities**

Everyone is entitled to the same ones, whatever race, gender or religion.

P is for **probation**

Typically, three excruciating months of being on your best behaviour.

Q is for **quarterly reviews**

These are also an opportunity to share your feedback in return.

R is for **redundancy**

If this happens, do some research – you have certain entitlements.

$ $ S is for **salary**

Don't settle for less than you're worth.

Z is for **zzz**

Make sure you get some.

Y is for **you're better than this**

If you hate your job, just leave.

X is for **remembering to save documents before closing the window**

W is for **work drinks**

Go to them once in a while.

V is for **very long days**

The average workday should be, but occasionally isn't, 9 to 5.

U is for **unpleasant schmucks**

Your office will have more of these than decent spoons.

T is for **tax returns**

Stressful, time-consuming, annoying. Prepare them well in advance.

What Are You Good At?

Age-old advice tells us to do what we love. While it's true that no one should ever give up on their passion, if it feels like you're not getting anywhere, it might be wise to pursue what you're good at, rather than what you obsess over.

If you're good at what you're passionate about, you've hit the jackpot.

A bad boss creates a culture that mimics from the top-down. There's a bit of a 'if you can't beat them, join them' attitude. It takes people a long time to recover from a bad boss. The positive? It teaches us how not to behave if we ever become a boss ourselves.

Kathleen Saxton is one of the leading UK advertising and media headhunters. She was recently named by Business Insider as one of the 'Top Global Media Recruiters Today'.

What Do You Want to Be ~~When You Grow Up?~~

Throughout childhood, everything points towards this all-important question. No wonder it fills us with anxiety when, as adults, we struggle to know what we want to do for a living. The problem with never becoming an astronaut or the president is that it sets us up to feel like failures. It's never too late to get that spacesuit. In fact, maybe it's a good thing to not know what you want to be. That way, nothing is off-limits.

Are You Telling the Whole Truth?

Get honest with yourself about what you want and what you aren't doing about it. You can't achieve something unless you're fully invested: heart, soul and all other bodily organs. Only then will you have the determination to stick it out when things get tough (and they most likely will).

It's no good saying 'I want to start a business' or 'I want to write a book' – that's easy. You don't get to own the noun without doing the verb.

Yes, good things come to those who wait, but they're far more likely to come to those who work really fucking hard to make them happen.

You Are Your Own Greatest Investment.

Whether it's some software, a gadget, a book or an online course, spending money on expanding your knowledge and skillset will never be wasted.

Don't Beat Yourself Up for What You Haven't Done Yet.

If you're spending time thinking about how bad you feel for not starting that business, visiting that country, writing that CV – that's wasted time. Stop dwelling, start doing.

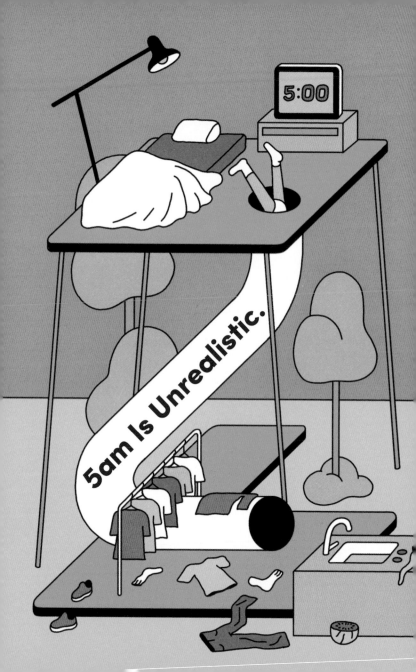

For the majority of us, 5am Pilates followed by positive affirmations, exfoliations, and papaya smoothies isn't going to happen. It's not *when* you wake up, but *how* you wake up that matters.

Don't Work for Free.

Internships are a great way of making new connections and gaining valuable experience. But beware of working for free. When you're starting out, you'll find people will ask for favours because 'it'll look good on your CV' or 'it's something to include in your portfolio'. The choice is yours, but just because you're inexperienced doesn't mean your time isn't worth something.

The C-Word.

'Career' belongs in the past, along with Trump, ballet pumps and mullets. The word implies you can't accept opportunities that are unrelated to the path you're currently on. It can imprison you, making you feel as though once you've made a decision, you can't veer away from it.

Just as over time we change as people, our ambitions (and haircuts) are allowed to change with us. How we approach the idea of 'having a career' is very different now compared to 20 years ago. If we could think of it as 'jumping between ladders', instead of climbing up the same one, that'd be more fitting.

You have
to reinvent yourself.
It's part of life. Dabbling
in different things breaks
up your life into these
really cool chapters. I like
to do a 'fuck it' every now
and then when it comes
to my career. It keeps
it interesting.

Adam Day-Lewin is a creative consultant for Twin London. He was previously Global Creative Director at Hearst Digital Media, home to *Esquire*, *Elle* and *Men's Health*. His past careers include drummer, set designer and club promoter.

You Will Be Disappointed.

Try not to get too emotionally invested in potential opportunities at the early stage when everything appears to be looking fantastic – whether it's the possibility of a job, potential deal or relationship. Often, something unexpected happens and everything goes swiftly downhill. Suddenly, the magnitude of disappointment matches that of your original optimism. It's good to reserve a bit of room for setbacks, and when things do go the way you'd hoped, you'll be that much more appreciative.

Stop Comparing Yourself to Others.

It's not the Olympics; this isn't a competition. You're the only one in your lane. Comparing your career path to others is not logical. That's like comparing a crab to a beluga whale; they're both sea creatures but that's about it.

Here's a metaphor for success that I made up: some people walk to work, some cycle, some may even helicopter there. They take different routes but eventually they will all arrive at their destination. See, we all have different journeys. We're all operating at different speeds.

The 10% Rule.

Every successful brand is constantly updating and improving itself; it's how they remain relevant. The monthly newsletters or the discount codes in your inbox are tactics businesses use to ensure consumers stay interested and don't forget about them.

You have to set aside time to think about what you're doing to enhance your brand and create opportunities for yourself. Dedicate 10 percent of every week to the brand of You. It might be writing an article, updating your website or reconnecting with an old boss, anything that lets people know you exist and you're worth knowing.

Don't be afraid of failing, often out of failures come great new ideas. Keep testing, learning and evolving. Try not to tackle too many things at once, it's better to focus on delivering five things brilliantly rather than ten badly.

Chrissie Rucker OBE is founder of The White Company, which she started in 1994 with £6,000 in savings. In 2020 the company posted an annual profit of over 14 million pounds. Describing herself as 'dyslexic, painfully shy and unacademic', Chrissie left school at 16 and, after spending time in magazines, launched The White Company aged just 24.

Never Say 'Think Outside the Box'.

What box? Why are you thinking inside a box? There are no excuses and no exceptions; if you catch yourself saying this you might as well lock yourself in a box and never come out.

Everyone's ~~a Game-Changing, Innovative, Disruptive, Amplifying Pioneer.~~ FAKING IT.

The moment powerful words are plucked from the dictionary and recycled into fashionable advertising talk for websites, radio ads and billboards (and consequently overused and abused by everyone) – they lose all their meaning. All their gravitas and grandeur is robbed from them and, just like that, nothing is truly 'amplifying' anymore (whatever that means, anyway).

Watch your words. Really consider what you're saying and avoid the predictable jargon and lazy clichés. Be mindful that your meaning doesn't become meaningless.

Fuck Up and Fail.

Make all the mistakes. You've got to be bad before you get good. The faster you fuck up, the faster you'll learn the lesson. Not fucking up is actually worse.

There's a lot more power in being young and naive than you might think. There's an ingrained arrogance that comes with age. They think they know it all, they think they've seen it all. They find it difficult to imagine a world they don't know. Naivety offers a different perspective, and it's so necessary. It's important to regularly practise being a beginner. Being the idiot in class really puts you in your place.

Sam Conniff is the best-selling author of *Be More Pirate* and Co-Founder of Livity UK. He is considered 'one of the sharpest minds on the planet' by Forbes. In 2020, Sam was invited by the Queen to receive an MBE for Services to Young People. He turned it down.

To: **neverstopdreaming2008@hotmail.com**
Subject: **Get a New Email Address**

If you're applying for jobs/communicating in general with the first email address you conceived at 12 years old, you must change it immediately. Stick to your own name. Email addresses are not an opportunity to get inventive.

You Are a Walking, Talking Billboard of You.

It takes under two seconds for someone to form an opinion of you, without you even opening your mouth. The pride you take in your appearance is a direct reflection of how much you value yourself and what you have to offer. Must I remind you to brush your hair (and teeth), trim your nails, wear deodorant and make a deliberate effort to look the part? All it takes is an extra few minutes before you walk out the door.

A holey T-shirt splattered with soy sauce stains isn't helping people take you seriously.

If you go into work and someone asks how you are, reply that you're 'Fucking great, thanks.' If someone asks if you can do something, say 'Of course I can!' Figure out how you'll actually do it later. Every time I do something, I feel like I'm blagging it, but after a while you start to realize you're just doing it.

Adam Day-Lewin is a creative consultant for **Twin London**, with clients including Rolex, Mercedes-Benz and Uniqlo. He openly admits to lying on his CV.

Don't Make Career Decisions Out of Desperation.

There are too many CVs filled with jobs people should never have accepted. During the height of my desperation and career confusion, I applied for a Christmas temp job in retail. I swore to myself (and made it very clear to everyone) that it was only for two months and I'd be gone by January. Before I knew it, two years had flown by and I was still selling bath bombs.

US€
YOUR TIM£
WI$ELY.

Time is the one thing you can't
get back. Consider it a currency
and spend it well.

Your Education Doesn't Mean Shit.

Glowing exam results, impressive qualifications, or the fact you were once Head Boy/Girl, do not decide how successful (or unsuccessful) you'll be later in life:

- **Rihanna**, a self-made billionaire, left school at 16.

- **Sir Richard Branson**, founder of the Virgin Group, dropped out of school at 16.

- **Jennifer Lawrence**, one of the highest-paid actresses in the world, left school at 14.

- **John Mackey**, founder of Whole Foods, dropped out of college six times.

- **Jay-Z**, a billionaire, dropped out of high school.

- **Travis Kalanick**, founder of Uber, dropped out of college.

- **Katy Perry** dropped out of school at 15 to pursue a music career.

- **Ralph Lauren** never finished his degree.

- **Steve Jobs, Steve Wozniak, Mark Zuckerberg, Bill Gates and Jack Dorsey** all dropped out of college.

See? Your education doesn't (necessarily) mean shit.

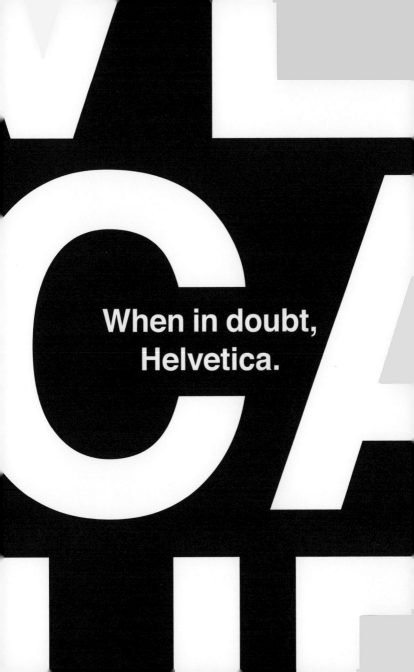

CV Dos

- Make sure it's no longer than one page.

- Include your contact details, not social handles.

- If you're including a blurb, turn it into bullet points.

- Always check for typos.

CV Don'ts

- If you've included 'Hello, nice to meet you', delete it.

- Any more than two colours and it starts to look like an art project.

- Don't share descriptions of what you did at that job, explain what you achieved.

FYI

- It's up to you if you want to include your home address, but I consider it an open invitation to stalkers.

- Everyone 'performs well under pressure' and 'thrives in a fast-paced environment'.

- If you're 'passionate' and a 'hard worker', that's great, but think of different ways to say it.

- People don't have time to read about your gap year in Australia, or the fact you swam for your local borough ten years ago. Keep it brief. This is for elite achievements only.

You Should (Probably) Privatize Your Social Accounts.

Apply for a job and they'll be doing a social media deep dive before they've got to the end of your cover letter. Within minutes, they'll be zooming in on photos from that all-inclusive hen do in Hvar five years ago. Having an open profile is risky business if you ask me.

High Intention, Low Expectation.

ON SUCCESS

"If there's something you want to learn, pursue and attack it in the most unconventional way, so it takes deep root in your soul. Keep goals short-term. The best strategy is high intention, low expectation. Remain as flexible as possible: your only concerns are the things you can control — your thoughts and actions."

ON DESTINY

"The narrative of 'believe in yourself, follow your heart, ignore the haters, follow your vision and you will have the destiny you choose', all that is the typical tale told by successful business gurus. But it's also a recipe for devastating failure. It completely ignores the role of fortune, of luck, of what life throws at you."

ON LUCK

"Develop your talent, develop the energy with which you get it out there and the rest is all luck. If you get the first two bits right, you're nudging the third bit to work in your favour."

"It's worth remembering that money makes you happier only to the point you don't have to worry about it. Beyond that amount, money does not make you happier the more you earn."

ADVICE TO MY YOUNGER SELF

Things pass, it's just one thing after another. Don't work so hard to impress people.

Derren Brown began his television career 20 years ago with a series called *Mind Control*. As well as being the master of manipulation, he is also the author of four books including the international bestseller *Happy*. In his spare time, Derren can be found painting portraits and baking butternut squash lasagne.

Assumption Is the Mother of All Fuckups.

Ask, clarify, ask again. Don't fall into the trap of nodding your head and pretending you've understood something when you haven't. It will come out, you will look silly and you will regret it. I should know.

You Are Not an Elephant.

Keep track of everything. Always take notes. This applies to shower thoughts, cooking thoughts, swimming thoughts, yoga thoughts. You are not an elephant; you will forget. There's nothing more annoying than the waiter who chooses not to write down your order to showcase how impressive their memory is. Quite often they get it wrong, and nearly always forget the extra side of fries. Don't be that cocky waiter.

Get Your Face Out of Your Phone.

The next time you're sitting on the bus or train, put your phone away. Take a mental note of the person sitting opposite you.

Consider who they might be, what their story is, what their interests are. Study the view outside.

Let your thoughts wander. Put YouTube in your pocket and observe reality instead.

Having an Opinion Is Important.

Having an opinion:

Shows you're passionate

Demonstrates critical thinking

Provokes healthy debates

Invites new discussions

Encourages others to share their own views

Not having an opinion:

Never leads anywhere interesting

Spot the Opportunity.

A chance meeting can lead to something.

At a restaurant a few years ago, the table next to me were laughing loudly about being on set for a film. I walked up to their table and told the man who I assumed was the director that I couldn't help but overhear their conversation. He invited me to join their table and we chatted for a while about the opportunities within the industry. He invited me on set the following day. The next morning I called in sick to work, outstayed my welcome and ended up at that film studio for over a year.

Another time at the dentist's, the woman waiting next to me looked interesting. I asked her what she did for a living. She gave me her business card, invited me for a coffee, and happened to be Sarah Doukas.

The 'Fuck It' Attitude.

THERE ARE NO PLAN BS

"I don't believe in Plan Bs. When I was young, I was indestructible. I had huge self-belief. If I was starting a company now, I'd have loads of reservations, but when you're young you just want to go for it. It's that 'fuck it' attitude, and you should embrace it while you can because you get too many people in your head as you get older and it makes you fearful."

STICK TO YOUR MISSION

"You can't give up at the first hurdle. When I decided to start my own company there were a lot of people telling me not to do it. I had a lot to lose but it didn't put me off. I think it would've discouraged a lot of people and they might've begun to feel unsure of themselves. I just had such a desire to do it for myself — not to be famous, not to make money — but to do something that I was proud of. I was on a mission."

SPEND MONEY WISELY

"Where you don't have expertise, get it from somewhere else. Don't blindly run into anything. Get the right advice. Especially for things you don't understand financially. You need to put in place great accountants and lawyers. Get yourself set up and remain cautious, especially with how you spend money. I didn't get a huge office, I wasn't flash; I wasn't spending loads of money."

I choose my team very wisely. I have people who have been with me for 25 years, I like to call them 'lifers'. It's important to keep a solid foundation of people who understand your vision. It's one thing being smart, but you need to have common sense. Treating people equally keeps you grounded, and you have to lead by example. It's important to be nice to everyone in all walks of life. It's a small world and I believe in good karma.

Sarah Doukas is the CEO and founder of Storm Management and one of the most influential people in the $2.4 trillion fashion industry. Formed in 1987, Storm is renowned for representing iconic faces, including Kate Moss, Anya Taylor-Joy and Cara Delevingne.

You Don't Have to Be Talented to Be Successful.
(BUT IT HELPS).

I'm sure there are many successful people in the public eye you consider to be 'talentless'. Although they may not appear to possess any obvious skills, what I guarantee they do have are copious amounts of dedication, tenacity, drive and motivation. Instead of developing a talent, they worked on developing a strong work ethic.

Newsflash: it's not always the most talented people who end up on top.

'A Big Fuck-Off Idea'.

Don't stress yourself out trying to come up with an idea that's never been done before. It's near impossible. Instead, you could start by focusing on adapting/ updating something that already exists. It's not stealing; it's creative borrowing.

You Don't Have to Be the Smartest in the Room.

YOU DIDN'T GO TO BUSINESS OR DESIGN SCHOOL, HOW HAVE YOU MADE THIS HAPPEN?

"I think it helped that I didn't have a traditional business or design education. Everything about how I started my company was atypical. At the time, new fashion brands started with one category and then tried to find a retailer to sell their clothes. Instead, I launched with multiple categories, our own store in Soho and our own website. People said I was crazy, but it worked. We had found white space in the market — I was making what was missing in my own closet, and what other women also wanted: beautiful, timeless pieces, below the traditional luxury price point."

WHAT'S YOUR BEST PIECE OF CAREER ADVICE?

"I have two: Embrace Your Ambition and Negativity is Noise. The first is about knowing where you want to go, setting your sights high and dreaming big dreams. The second is about knowing who to listen to and who to ignore. Constructive criticism from people you respect is so important, but negativity is always an unhelpful distraction."

"Resilience is essential – and for me that's about hope and optimism, trusting that even if things are difficult now, something better could be just around the corner. Clear values are so important; when you know what you stand for it's easier to stay on track when things get tough. And a little courage can take you a long way. Everyone hates cold calling, no one likes networking with strangers, but making connections makes all the difference."

WHAT IS KEY TO MAINTAINING
A SUCCESSFUL GLOBAL BRAND?

Trust your gut and do everything with integrity.

Tory Burch was listed by Forbes as one of 'The World's 100 Most Powerful Women' in 2020, the same year that *Newsweek* recognized her label as one of '50 US Businesses That Stood Out During the Pandemic'. The Tory Burch brand has an approximate value of $1.5 billion.

Know What's Going On.

Have a vague idea of what's happening in the world, so you don't look like an ignorant airhead.

It's important to contribute to topical discussions that happen in the common room, around the coffee machine, in meeting rooms. You don't have to understand the world of politics, or what's going on in the pharmaceutical industry, but it's wise to pick up a paper once in a while or visit a news website* and take a glance at the basic world overview. It's foolish to avoid the headlines, no matter how depressing they might be.

*NEVER THE SUN, DAILY MAIL, PEOPLE OR US WEEKLY. THESE DON'T COUNT.

Don't Be a Thieving Bastard.

Steal someone else's idea and it'll come back to bite you. It's called creative karma, bitch.

There Are Lots of Bad Bosses Out There.

Just because they're your boss, doesn't mean they're a good role model or leader. Shitty bosses lead to unhappy employees and unhealthy work environments. If your office has issues you can usually point to the people at the top. There's something about authority going to a person's head, metamorphosing them into bad-tempered bastards on a power trip.

WFH: Working From Hell?

Personally, a typical day working from home involves sitting in the same spot for hours, little to no fresh air and copious amounts of caffeine. Sometimes I don't change out of my pyjamas until 6pm. Articles about a healthy working-from-home routine might tell you the following:

- **Set your alarm for the same time every day.**

- **Have a shower.** Put the cold tap on, then the hot one, then make it freezing.

- **Eat a nutritious breakfast** comprised of chia seeds, goji berries and protein.

- **Do something productive** in the time you would've spent on your commute.

- **Create a welcoming workspace.** Get a desk plant.

- **Stretch often.**

- **Surround yourself** with nuts and crudités.

- **Get out** of the house and go for an afternoon walk.

Working from home might seem like a lovely idea but it can be a real challenge both mentally and physically. As long as you get a good amount of sleep, take frequent breaks and maintain some level of routine, you should be alright. There's no right or wrong approach, as long as you're getting the work done.

Mole-in-a-Hole.

You know the game where you have to whack a mole on the head with a mallet when it pops out from its hole? Next time you have any negative, self-deprecating, sabotaging thoughts, think of them like those little moles. Whack them away, one at a time.

Aim to be good at two things, rather than excellent at one thing. Don't just rely on what you do, have one or two complementary disciplines; this is your hinterland*.

If you're trying to be the best X in the world, you're almost certainly going to fail because there are thousands of other people trying to do the same. But if you try and become the best X in the world who can also do Y, then a) it will be easier to become distinctive and noticed and b) opportunities will come your way. It's easier to be the best person in the world at two things, simply through mathematical probability.

*Hinterland: noun: an area lying beyond what is visible or known.

Rory Sutherland is Vice-Chairman of Ogilvy UK.
He is regarded as one of the most influential advertising professionals in the world.

People Will Judge You.

People will always find something not to like. So, you might
as well embrace everything about yourself, flaws and all.
You do you sweetie, haters gonna hate.

People will judge you because of your age.
People will judge you because of your gender.
People will judge you because of your race.
People will judge you because of your sexuality.
People will judge you because of your religion.
People will judge you because of your beliefs.
People will judge you because of your weight.
People will judge you because of your height.
People will judge you because of your intelligence.
People will judge you because of your accent.
People will judge you because of your education.
People will judge you because of your postcode.
People will judge you because of your money.
People will judge you because of your lack of money.
People will judge you because of your music taste.
People will judge you because of your hobbies.
People will judge you because of your tattoos.
People will judge you because of your hair colour.
People will judge you because of your haircut.
People will judge you because of your confidence.
People will judge you because of your lack of confidence.
People will judge you because you're too nice.
People will judge you because of your shoes.
People will judge you because you've got a social life.
People will judge you because you haven't got a social life.
People will judge you because of your love of country music.
People will judge you because of the length of your nails.
People will judge you because of your packed lunch.
People will judge you because you prefer dogs.

Pay Attention
to the Small Things.

Duvet Days.

Sometimes the idea of going into work might be too unbearable. When this happens, I suggest you call in sick, take the day off and stay in bed. Every once in a while, we must all succumb to a 'severe bout of food poisoning' or a 'chronic migraine'.

This, my friends, is a healthy white lie. It's just another way of making sure you're looking after yourself. And, don't feel guilty; everyone does it at some point.

RIDE THE WAVES.

Try not to attach too much weight to 'discovering your purpose.' It's normal to not know what you're doing with your life. For some people it's constantly changing, and for others it doesn't come until much later down the road. We'd all like to get there faster, but most of us just have to zip up the wetsuit and ride the waves of uncertainty.

Work Is Not Life.

You need to establish some boundaries, or your work life will start merging into your personal life. Consider these strategies:

- **At home, keep work devices in a different room.** If it's not a crucial notification, don't open it.

- **If it is possible to turn your work devices off, do it.**

- **You don't have to accept** your colleagues' friend requests on Facebook, Instagram or LinkedIn.

- **If you're working from home, allocating meeting slots will give you control over your diary.** If you don't do this, you run the risk of always being at people's beck and call, agreeing to all meetings, at any time, with little notice.

- **If you're not in the mood, skip the work drinks.**

be

wary

of giving

your

personal

number

to

colleagues

suddenly

you'll be

texting about work

until

midnight

and

replying to emails

on Saturdays

Give Your Brain a Break.

Remove yourself from the glare
of the computer. Give yourself a facial.
Crack your knuckles. Do a crossword.
Take the dog for a walk. Have a bath.
Make a drink (with or without gin).

1	2	3	4	5		6	7
■	8	G	E	T	9		
10				■	11 O	F	F
12 ⊗	T	I	K	13	■	14	
15		■	16	T	17 O	K	
18		19	■	20			
21			22				■
23		■	24				

GET CRITICAL.

ASK WHAT'S

WRONG

WITH SOMETHING,
NOT WHAT'S

RIGHT

Don't Be a Stale Ham Sandwich.

Tasteless, dry, bland. Don't be a stale ham sandwich when you can be a fajita – fiery, fun, flavourful.

If you live every day of your life the same way, making the same decisions and plans, you leave no room for excitement or surprise. Things will quickly turn boring and predictable. Say 'Yes' more. Give in to new experiences and opportunities.

'Content' is a shit word. It literally means 'stuff'. It's a shorthand word that covers so many different things. When people say 'We need to create digital content' what they really mean is they want to create a video on YouTube. No one says 'I'm going home to watch content' or 'I read some great content today.' Content creators, what do they do? They make stuff. They should call themselves Creators of Stuff.

Vikki Ross is an award-winning copywriter. She has worked with major global brands including Sky, Twitter and Spotify.

Don't Be a
Negative Nancy.

A positive approach works wonders
for productivity. Mindset is everything.
Embrace a 'can-do' attitude.

You Have Two Ears.

If you've got nothing constructive or crucial to say in a meeting, don't say it. There's much more to be gained by keeping your mouth shut, no matter how much you like the sound of your own voice.

You have the right to remain silent. Practise being better at listening than speaking.

Be a Coffee Bitch.

Making people tea and coffee at work isn't a sign of weakness, it's a nice thing to do. But make sure you're more than just the person who makes the hot drinks.

JUST SAY THANKS

When someone pays you a compliment,
whether it's about your scent, shoes
or skills, just smile and say, 'Thanks.'
Whether you agree or not doesn't matter.

Don't Be Afraid of the Phone.

The office is silent. The phone rings. Everyone turns to look at you, their eyes burning into your soul, fingers frozen, suspended above keyboards. Well, are you going to answer? Your hands turn clammy, your throat is dry. They're still staring, mouths agape. What's my name? What's the greeting?

The way you answer a call is important; you're meant to say something. It's amazing how many people remain silent. This is extremely odd behaviour, and you must stop doing it.

Clear your throat. A feeble 'hello' is not the best way to start a conversation; confidence and clarity, please. And smile. The other person will be able to hear it in your voice.

Get a Mentor.

They can be an old boss, someone who's in a field you're interested in, or a person whose career you admire. They're usually someone who has walked your path before and is able to guide you through its rocky terrain. A mentor will help you explore career options, set goals, motivate you and broaden your contacts.

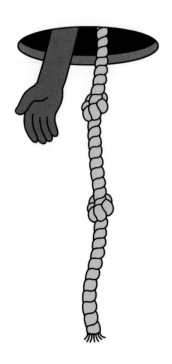

Rules are 90 percent conventions, habits and sticking plasters on people's mistakes. It's your responsibility to break them. Pick a rule, break it, and replace it with a better one. When you show up to a new job, you might think your main task is to fit in — it's not. It's a mistake to try to be a chameleon. You shouldn't follow the patterns and footsteps of people before you. The opposite is true.

Sam Conniff is the writer and director of *Uncertainty Experts,* the world's first interactive documentary, scientifically proven to increase resilience and decrease anxiety. He also happens to be my old boss.

Use People.

Make use of the resources in your office. Need help designing a logo or some insight on a particular subject? You needn't look too far. Always start with your colleagues; you'll usually find someone in the building is an expert.

Don't Let the Good Ones Get Away.

Stay in touch with former colleagues and old bosses. Keep track of what they're up to. Invite them for a coffee once in a while and make use of their expertise. It's sort of like career counselling. Just because they're from your past, doesn't mean they can't help in the future.

Don't Be a Dick.

People who act like total dicks are gaining nothing from their stinky attitude. These people go about their dickish daily lives oblivious to the display of middle fingers targeted behind their backs.

It's simple; be equally pleasant to everyone, from the window cleaner, to the receptionist, to the boss. If you're a crappy person, people will spot it immediately. They'll start avoiding you, you'll grow deep wrinkles and develop a permanent sour taste in your mouth. Worst of all, you'll end up alone and miserable with no one to attend your funeral.

Spot the Influencer.

In every office there's an influencer;
someone who everyone likes, and confides
in, and whose opinion is respected.
Often, they're not in a position of power.
Make an effort to get to know them.

People Care Less Than You Think.

You can never guarantee success. But the truth is that if you stand still, you get left behind. You need to be restless, to be bold, to take risks. That's what keeps you relevant.

HOW LONG DID IT TAKE FROM HAVING THE IDEA TO LAUNCHING YOUR FIRST PRODUCT?

"I came up with PROPERCORN in 2009. I was hoping to crack it in a few months. Instead, it took a couple of years. I made my first batches of popcorn in a cement mixer in my mum's kitchen and used a car-spraying kit for the oil. It wasn't until 2011 that I partnered with my co-founder Ryan Kohn, and we took our first product to market."

WHAT WAS THE BIGGEST CHALLENGE?

"Moving into a fiercely male industry. The first year was by far the hardest. By the end of it, I felt deflated, patronized, lonely. It was a real lesson in resilience, and I'm stronger for it."

WHAT HAVE YOU LEARNT?

"In the early years I struggled with insecurities about being a woman in business. My mum eventually called me out and said, 'Who do you think you are? People aren't going home dissecting everything you've done. They don't go home with you on their mind. They have their own shit to deal with.' And she was right. People care less than you think."

HAVE YOU EVER CONSIDERED QUITTING?

"When I was starting out, I was told by an industry bigwig that I should ask for my old job back. I remember he told me that 'the big boys are coming'. It was disheartening, but it made me more determined than ever to be successful. Expect to be knocked back. If you're passionate and focused on your goal, you'll win over the sceptics."

Cassandra Stavrou MBE is the Co-Founder of PROPER Snacks, the UK's largest independent snack brand, selling over 5 million bags every month. In 2020, she was awarded an MBE for her Services to the Food Industry.

Things You Need to Stop Saying.

'Basically', 'literally' and 'if that makes sense' are not helping you.

Things You're Guaranteed to Start Saying (Whether You Like It or Not).

Even if it goes against all your morals, you'll soon begin to adopt office jargon.

Suddenly you're asking for things before the 'end of play', you're beginning sentences with 'going forward', you're 'touching base', asking Janet to 'ping' it over and wondering what the 'ETA' is.

Fight it all you want but you won't win this battle.

Clients Don't Know What They Want.

Get used to this. Their opinions might be illogical, contradictory and temperamental. Like a plane with no destination, you might find yourself aimlessly going around in circles. Why don't you try asking what they don't want, rather than what they do?

Don't lose your cool, put your ego aside and remember they're paying your bills.

Dolly Parton Was Lying.

Be prepared to work longer than 9 to 5. Having to work extra hours is part of the job. There will be days where you'll have to eat lunch at your desk, or you'll have to get the last train home and cancel dinner plans. Sometimes, you might find your office feels more familiar than your home.

Occasionally, you must be willing to make the odd exception outside your normal work hours. Deadlines, last-minute meetings, international calls, spreadsheets – they don't stop being important after 5pm.

Help.

Never be afraid to ask someone for support. In the unlikely event they say no, simply blacklist them from your life and never acknowledge their existence again.

The job is to do the right thing for the client, not the right thing for your creativity. Put your romantic ideas aside and say what you need to say in the most effective way. If you're going to argue, do it as if you are presenting a case in court — it must be balanced and measured, not emotional.

Vikki Ross is a copywriter* named one of the 'Top 100 trailblazers redefining the creative industry' by The Dots.

*A COPYWRITER IS SOMEONE WHO WRITES WORDS FOR ADVERTISING. 'COPY' IS THE TEXT ITSELF. 'JUST DO IT', 'TASTE THE RAINBOW', 'FINGER LICKIN' GOOD' — THESE WERE ALL CONCEIVED BY COPYWRITERS. A COPYWRITER IS NOT SOMEONE WHO WRITES THE TERMS AND CONDITIONS. THEY DON'T HAVE A LEGAL BONE IN THEIR BODY.

No One Likes Small Talk.

If you're an anxious person who finds social situations traumatic, the good news is you don't have to network, not in the traditional sense, anyway.

'Networking' doesn't have to mean standing awkwardly in a room full of strangers, nervously clutching a warm beer and your freshly printed business cards. There are plenty of other ways to get someone's attention. Initiate a conversation on your own terms – send emails, arrange a virtual coffee. Be seen at things. Get to know your boss outside the office. What does Ray in accounts do in his spare time? What's the name of Lynda's dog? People love talking about themselves, so give them the opportunity to do just that.

It's (semi) true what they say – it's not what you know, but who you know – so get to know people.

* *

HOLD ON TO YOUR RECEIPTS

* *

No matter how organized you think
you are, buy a folder to safely
store receipts and tickets.

If you don't, a month later,
when you have to do your expenses,
you'll have misplaced them.

Suddenly, your company-paid
trip to Legoland wasn't
so fun after all.

* *

TOTAL DAMAGE   £143.48

* *

Shake It,
Shake It Real Good.

You can judge a human by their handshake. If you've got a weak one, this is you choosing to communicate to the world that you are the human equivalent of wilted spinach.

1. Make eye contact.

2. Tell them your name.

3. Be firm.

4. Give their hand a small squeeze, don't limply leave yours hovering against theirs – no one wants a delicate caress.

5. Ensure your handshake lasts at least two seconds. Anything less and you'll look like you're frightened of commitment.

* Trim your nails.

* Sweaty palms? Wipe them discreetly on the nearest fabric surface.

* Don't wrap your index finger around theirs; that's for cults and Freemasons only.

Or perhaps physical contact in this post-pandemic world doesn't sit right with you. In which case, a friendly smile and wave is sufficient. Save the elbow bumps for friends, not potential future bosses.

Scamp.

When communicating an idea, an unpolished one is better than a perfectly executed one. If it's got potential, people will get it straight away.

A 'scamp' is a very simple doodle. It's used in advertising to showcase an idea for a product or advert quickly and effectively, without wasting time perfecting it. It's usually done on an A4 piece of paper with a thick black felt tip. It should only take a minute or two.

Draw a border around the page to create a frame, turn it landscape and do a shitty little drawing within it. The amount of detail should be just enough for people to recognize it and give their own input.

1. What's the idea?

2. Why does it need to be made now?

3. Who's it for?

4. Why should you be the one to make it?

5. How will you do it?

6. Where will it exist (online, on paper, on the side of a bus)?

7. What could it evolve into?

If you can answer these questions, you can sell it. When we sell ideas, we can get muddled in all the small details. Sometimes we forget, what's the core offering here? You've got to be sensitive to the person you're pitching to. Don't assume you know what they're looking for.

Luke Hyams is YouTube's first Head of Originals for Europe, the Middle East and Africa. He was previously Director of Global Content at The Walt Disney Company.

Manners Maketh Man (and Woman).

PLEASE.

Just because you're not six years old staying over at a friend's house doesn't make manners any less important. In fact, they're more relevant as an adult.

THANK YOU.

Never Bitch About Your Last Job/Boss/Office in an Interview.

Firstly, you don't know who the interviewer might know, and secondly, it will make them question if one day you'll do the same about them. Either way, it's not a good idea.

It's OK to Be Annoying
... SOMETIMES.

If you really want someone's attention, stopping at sending that one email is not good enough. Important people are busy; you can't just give up. This is the part where pride goes out the window. You must persevere and keep on trying. Find another way in. Just don't get weird with it. When the police come knocking at your door, that's when you've probably gone too far.

'Janet,
You're on Mute.'

Microphone issues, awkward exits, shitty wi-fi. Meetings online rarely run smoothly.

- **Don't be like Janet.** Make sure you've pressed unmute when it's your turn to talk.

- **Dress your bottom half.** Putting on a shirt with no pants is not a good idea. Your doorbell will ring, and you'll forget about your state of undress. Before you know it, you've exposed your derrière to a handful of work colleagues and it's time to hand in your notice.

- **Prepare to ninja-tap.** When you're ready to leave the meeting, hover your cursor over the exit button in advance (sometimes you have to press twice).

- **Inform others** in your household that a work call is about to take place. You don't want your mum popping up asking what you want for dinner.

- **Make yourself aware** of the 'share screen' button and avoid accidentally pressing it.

Might I suggest investing in a slidey gadget to cover your webcam? It'll help with the inevitable wave of paranoia that comes with exiting a video meeting.

Dust Yourself Off.

Get back on that horse. Anything worth doing doesn't come easy. Your mother didn't raise a quitter.

FUCK THIS
FUCK HER
FUCK YOU
FUCK HIM
FUCK THEM
FUCK MY LIFE
FUCK OFF
FUCK ME
FUCK THAT
FUCK THIS JOB
FUCK. ←—— YOUR NEW FAVOURITE WORD.

Ten Minutes in Front of the Computer Is Not Lunch.

This is Frank. Frank sits at his computer all day. His posture is appalling. He is stressed and tired. He needs a holiday, and a massage. For lunch, Frank unwraps his homemade sandwich and eats it at his desk, simultaneously tapping away at his keyboard. This is Frank's lunch, and it's over within minutes. He wipes his mouth, scrunches up his napkin, brushes the crumbs off his lap on to the floor, and returns to work.

There are many simple pleasures in this world, and your lunch break is one of them. Behaving in this way is disrespectful to yourself, and your sandwich. Don't be like Frank.

'Good Job.'

Telling someone they did a 'good job' when in fact it was an 'average job' might seem like an encouraging thing to do, but it's dangerous territory and is of no substance whatsoever. Stop doing it. The more you tell people they have done well when they haven't, the lower the bar is set and the lazier they will become. It's actually counterproductive. Give credit where credit's due and reward others when they deserve it.

No Thanks, Hun.

Things to avoid including in work emails:

'Hun', 'babe', or 'love' should
be reserved for loved ones only.

Capitalizing words and sentences.
WHY ARE YOU SHOUTING, WHAT'S WRONG?

You never need two question marks
in a row. Just how desperately
curious are you?

Don't ever place two exclamation
marks next to each other. One will
do the job just fine.

Smiley faces. Best steer clear of these
if you don't know your audience.

Typos. We don't want any
'breast wishes'.

Never Say the F-Word.

Companies that refer to themselves as a 'family' are usually disguising something. This is most likely code for 'everyone's secretly miserable and our culture is toxic'. It's a clever leadership tactic, leading to employees working for free on weekends and staying beyond their contracted hours, all in the name of family loyalty. Businesses are nothing like families because:

Jobs are not permanent

You can get fired or replaced at any time

You're getting paid in exchange for a skill

**There are certain standards
you must adhere to**

While the analogy might appear inviting, it's inappropriate and it's not cute.

Google Doesn't Have the Answer.

wh

what is the meaning of life

what is the purpose of a human being

why do i exist

Don't Bring Your Favourite Mug into the Office.

It will go missing.

If You Don't Want to Put Money Towards Their Birthday Present ... Don't.

It's always someone's birthday in an office. Sometimes, you won't like the person. In this case, don't feel pressured to contribute to their spa day or gift voucher. Bid them a 'happy birthday', sign the card and merrily get on with your day.

happy birthday

HAPPY BIRTHDAY LOVELY! NEVER SPOKEN TO YOU IN MY LIFE. HAVE THE BEST DAY EVER! XO

happy Birthday

HAVE A GREAT DAY! XX

113 YEARS OLD TODAY!

Please See Attached. Get into the habit of double-checking that a) you have actually included the 'attached' and b) it's the correct file. Sending a follow-up email acknowledging your mistake is always painful.

Presentations Are Never Fun.

You can't escape them; they're like a (evil) rite of passage. Few people in the world can wing them with zero preparation – you're probably not one of them.

1. Save all the necessary files in the correct order and under the correct names.

2. Don't forget your USB, chargers, adapters, clickers – the last thing you want is to waste time fiddling around with cables and getting yourself into a hot sweaty mess.

3. Spend the ten minutes leading up to your presentation/meeting/pitch shifting your mindset into a positive realm of self-belief. Visit the loo. Gather your thoughts. Stare into the mirror. Speak kind words to your reflection. Slap yourself.

4. Be the first in the room. Get accustomed to your surroundings.

5. Greet people as they enter, make small talk, thank them for coming.

6. Don't make any self-deprecating comments – no 'I'm really bad at these'-type statements.

The good thing is that people don't want you to feel bad about your mediocre performance. They'll tell you that you did a great job, regardless of your shit show.

Typos.

If there's a typo in your document or email, there are a lot of people ~~that~~ *WHO* won't be forgiving. You might have a fantastic idea or a strong proposal but the moment someone spots a misspelt word, the value of your work diminishes. It will convey that you don't pay close a*T*tention to detial, and you take little pride in *YOUR* ~~you're~~ work. A spelling error can be the difference between someone else getting the job over you.

THE

MOMENT

YOU START GETTING

COMPUTER
HEADACHES,

THAT'S WHEN YOU NEED

TO GET AN EYE TEST.

You Can't Shake a Shitty Reputation.

Give yourself a bad name and it will stick with you for life. What people think of you and how you conduct yourself really matters. It's a small world, people love to gossip, and it won't take long for the word to get around.

On the flip side, having a good reputation works wonders – people will want to help you and opportunities will come your way simply because a) you're good at what you do and b) you're a pure delight.

You're Not the Centre of the Universe.

You are merely one of 7.8 billion multicellular organisms, floating around the planet feeding off particles and things and trying to survive another day. For what reason? We'll never know.

Tips for Not Losing Your Goddamn Mind.

- **Try not to eat lunch at your desk.**

- **Don't get involved** in office drama.

- **Headphones are handy** for drowning out the voices of people you hate.

- **Keep your desk tidy.**

- **Stay hydrated**; it's good for you and it forces you to take loo breaks (= time away from your computer).

- **Try to remain calm** if your lunch disappears from the fridge (it will).

If you do this, then maybe
it's time to call it quits.

- AVOID TELLING PEOPLE WHAT
  YOU DO OR WHERE YOU WORK

- FIND THAT YOU'RE ENVIOUS
  OF OTHER PEOPLE'S ROLES
  AND CAREERS

- MAKE UP EXCUSES TO CALL
  IN SICK

- EXPERIENCE AN OVERWHELMING
  SENSE OF DREAD ON A SUNDAY

Don't worry, your colleagues won't miss
you *that* much, you *are* replaceable,
and pretty soon after your goodbye
prosecco and communally signed card,
they'll unfriend you on LinkedIn.

The A-Ha! Myth.

The supposed flash-of-genius lightbulb moments that people seem to have aren't as spontaneous as they might appear. There's a lengthy process that happens before that bit and it can be broken down into these four stages:

1. GO FORAGING

Take time gathering information. Find out all you can about whatever it is you're working on. Fill your brain with facts. Become a guru on that specific product/ business/subject/brand. Make it your mission to know it inside out.

2. LET IT MARINATE

Just like a good Bolognese, the longer you leave information stewing in your noggin, the better the outcome. Let your newfound knowledge simmer. It might be hours. Maybe weeks. Switch off from the subject. You've done all your research and now you must allow it to bubble away beneath the surface as you concentrate on other things. Like the washing up.

3. SPECIAL DELIVERY

The 'A-ha!' moment. The part where a masterpiece arrives in your brain, fully formed, like it's been hand-delivered by the Ideas Factory. Everything slots together beautifully and you can finally stop biting your nails and crying into your keyboard. This exquisite moment might strike when you're in the shower, or at 3am mid-dream. It happens when the marinading is complete.

4. LIFT OFF!

This is the part where you need to be your own worst critic. Play devil's avocado and rip the idea to shreds. Question everything. Ask yourself things like, is it relevant? Does it solve the issue? Start again if you have to.

If genius isn't striking, just keep foraging.

Don't Take Yourself Too Seriously.

KEEP IT AUTHENTIC

"For a business to work, you need shared values: drive, vision, culture, authenticity — these things need to come from the inside. You can't hire consultants; it has to come from the founders or the management — right from the core. Think about IKEA — we all get the idea; anyone might copy them, but they can't. Why? Because the fundamentals exist within the company."

DEFINE YOUR FOCUS

"What gives you the right to exist as a company, as a brand in the world? If you can define that and make it clear, then everything becomes easier. What are the key elements that you want to provide to consumers? Identify the three most important things and where the focus should be."

UNLEARN AND RELEARN

"Be fearless and adaptable — you need to be able to unlearn and relearn, constantly. It's more about the ability to adapt than it is about making great plans. Plans will always change."

"You can have a fantastic product, but it has to be relevant and it has to be interesting. It can't just be one or the other. Oatly existed for 25 years before it started to gain awareness. The issue was because the product was only relevant to people who were lactose intolerant. We removed all the scientific claims on the front of the packaging. We did it because we realized that information wasn't relevant to our audience who were not lactose intolerant. What was more important to us was to use our packaging to talk about who we are, to tell our story."

PUT THINGS IN PERSPECTIVE

Don't take yourself too seriously. Embrace failure. So, you made a mistake – did anyone die? No? Then learn from it and move on.

Toni Petersson is the CEO of Oatly and 'the man responsible for making oat milk a thing'. Founded in the 1990s, Oatly struggled to gain a market. Toni joined as CEO in 2012. As of 2020, Oatly is worth over $2 billion.

I'm Not Crying, You're Crying.

A great idea has the power to influence and change behaviour. In order to believe in something, you have to feel something. If you feel something, you're more likely to do something. Take voting, for example.

At the heart of all great work is emotion. It needs to move you. That's the only way you'll connect to it, remember it and act upon it. In everything you do, search for how you might be able to squeeze out the emotion, whether it's joy, sadness, surprise or anger.

Complete the Damn Task.

Don't leave things half-finished.*

Learning to finish things is just as much about self-discipline and commitment as it is about enjoying the final product. Completing anything challenging will always make you proud of yourself. The experience is the real achievement.

*JIGSAW PUZZLES, BOOKS, CUPS OF TEA; THEY'RE ALL BETTER FINISHED.

Should I Give Up, or Should I Just Keep Chasing ~~Pavements?~~
PAYMENTS?

The answer is no, never give up. Particularly if you're freelance, invoices often get forgotten, or paid late. Don't be shy. As uncomfortable as it might feel, if you are owed money for a service you provided, you must make people aware, but presume it's an honest mistake.

Be More Duck.

Calm on the surface, frantically paddling
for dear life underneath.

Don't do what you think is trendy or fashionable or what you think people want to see. Make work that makes you the happiest. If you do that, hopefully other people will like it as well and then you'll get to enjoy what you do and it won't feel like 'work'.

Mr Bingo is an artist and public speaker.
His work has been featured in the *Financial Times*, *New York Times* and *Guardian*. In 2015, he launched the most successful Kickstarter campaign for a book in the UK. It was around this time that he promised never to work for clients again.

Speak Up, Buttercup.

You'll always remember the rebellious one in school who was continuously in detention, who voiced their opinions and challenged the teachers. But can you recall the quiet ones who always complied, never spoke up and always did their homework on time? (No offence to them, I'm sure they're very successful in life.)

Following the crowd is lame. Blending in is boring. Care passionately about what matters to you and project it proudly.

Get a Move On.

When you're overwhelmed by choice, the best thing you can do is make one. If you have no direction or goal in mind, the first step is to do something. Anything.

LIKE PEOPLE, SUCCESS COMES IN ALL

SHAPES

AND

SIZES

It's Cool to Be Proud of Yourself.

Sharing your success is part of the reward of hard work and it should never feel like boasting.

If those around you make you feel guilty or ashamed for tooting your own horn, then you might want to explore new friendship horizons. Don't be sheepish, you deserve to be proud of your accomplishments. The same goes for praising others for their achievements too; don't be stingy.

Become a Spy.

Take note of the people in your life who are achieving their goals and learn from them. Talk to them about their experiences and ask for their advice and guidance. Observing others is also a good way to model what not to do.

You Can't Expect Everyone to Like You.

Some of the best things in existence divide opinion. Perhaps you're one of them.

I believe *Mrs Doubtfire* is one of the greatest films of all time; some people would disagree. (I hate them because of it, but that's not the point.)

Public Speaking.

Hated by many, loved by literally no one. Whatever the scenario:

- **Water.** Keep a glass nearby (to combat 'dry mouth', a gift from Mother Nature).

- **Avoid coffee.** Nerves and caffeine are not a wise combination.

- **Take your time.** Pause often.

- **Maintain eye contact with your audience.** If you're really struggling, select one person in the room and commit to them (visually, not romantically).

- **Don't say 'D'you know what I mean?'** If you feel the urge to ask it, chances are what you're saying is unclear. Instead, ask if anyone has a question.

- **Embrace the silence.**

- **Props help.** Consider holding a drink or some notes. If your mind goes blank, pause and take a sip of your drink.

- **Tech.** If what you're doing involves tech, make sure you've prepared and tested all equipment.

- **Don't picture your audience naked.** It's distracting and requires far too much imagination.

- **Remember: no one gives a shit about you.** The likelihood is no one's even listening.

Sometimes It Only Takes a Minute.

Don't feel discouraged if the best idea you have is the first one.

Bigger Is Not Better.

Once upon a time, I was in a long, tedious meeting with clients of the particularly indecisive variety. We'd been going around in circles discussing campaign ideas for months, much like a teacup ride – we were getting nowhere, and we were starting to feel nauseous. Leaping out of his seat, as if believing he had solved a world crisis, the client proclaimed, 'How about we just make the logo bigger?' The graphic designer, eyes bulging out of their sockets, nostrils flaring, responded by grabbing the nearest pencil and frantically scribbling the word 'wanker' in tiny letters on the bottom of a piece of paper.

In other words, if the idea is shit, making the logo bigger isn't going to disguise that. Something doesn't need to be screaming in your face for it to provoke a reaction.

WANKER

Milk It.

Think of opportunities
as cows, and milk them for
all they're worth. Personally,
I like to always outstay
my welcome.

Be so good that they don't
want to see you go.

Be More Bee.

Twenty percent of bees don't obey the waggle dance (how they tell each other where to find food and water). These 'rebel' bees choose instead to explore the areas where most of the bees aren't going. If every bee obeyed the waggle dance the hive would get trapped in a local maximum. What would be the benefit in 100 percent of the bees exploring the same area day in and day out?

Without the 20 percent of rogue explorer bees, the hive would never discover anything new and it wouldn't be capable of adapting.

It's OK to do your own thing, that's where discovery and new ideas happen. So, be more (rogue) bee.

Aim to Get Better Every Day.

HOW DO YOU GET BETTER IF YOU'RE CONSIDERED THE BEST?

One of the weirdest things from a chef's perspective is, we're only as good as people think we are. Everything is based on reputation. You can never think you're the best at anything because it doesn't exist; it's all a perception.

WHAT MAKES YOU GOOD AT WHAT YOU DO?

"Determination, perseverance and hard work. I'm in the constant pursuit of excellence. I have an obsessive nature for detail, and I have tremendous professional pride. I put everything into my work because I don't see it as work — it's a lifestyle choice. I'm tough on myself because I care so much; there's a fragility that comes with wanting to do something perfectly."

I'm always bothered about what other people think. With food critics, I remember every single word someone has ever written about me, but I use it as fuel to prove them wrong.

ARE YOU IN COMPETITION WITH YOURSELF?

"I have to get better every day. It can be a tiny little thing, but it has to be an improvement. If you're always evolving and always moving forward, you will always be getting better. I never take a step back, I can't stand still; if you're standing still, you're moving backwards."

Clare Smyth MBE is the first and only British female chef to hold three Michelin stars, for her restaurant, Core by Clare Smyth, in London. It holds a 10/10 score in the Good Food Guide and 5/5 AA rosettes. She was named the 'World's Best Female Chef' by the World's 50 Best Restaurants in 2018.

Remove the Juju.

Get rid of all the negative elements stopping you from being more focused or content. This could be people, relationships or environments.

They say you are an amalgamation of the five people you spend the most time with, so now is your opportunity to assess those characters closely and distance yourself where necessary. The chances are, if these people are sucking the joy out of their own lives like a human Hoover, they're doing the same to yours. Surround yourself with people you admire, respect and want to emulate. Their qualities will rub off on you. For free.

You Will Get Rejected.

Rejection is a part of life. It belongs in the same category as heartbreak and hair loss; no one wants it, but it's unavoidable.

The proposal for this book received 41 rejection emails. For fun (and not because I'm bitter), here are some of the responses I got:

```
'While you write very well,
    we were not captivated'

'I am sure that this could be intriguing,
    but I did not feel a connection
            to your work'

    'This is honest and amusing,
  but I'm afraid it's just not for us'
```

Rejection should not discourage you. Confront the ways you could try harder, or approach things differently. Be your own critic. Don't dwell on why it didn't happen, but on how you can make it happen.

Today, a Van Gogh painting is worth £100 million. Throughout his lifetime, he sold next to nothing. He died poor and unknown. Rejection is not always a reflection of your skill, it's sometimes just plain old bad timing.

Big D* Energy.

Everyone questions themselves, even Oprah. You'll never know if you never try.

* DOUBT.

Are you neglecting your relationship because you're so consumed with work? Do you find yourself cancelling on plans with friends in favour of staying in the office to finish that really important thing?

If this happens more than you'd like, or more than it should, either:

A) INVITE YOUR FRIENDS
   TO YOUR OFFICE FOR
   A SLEEPOVER

B) RE-EVALUATE YOUR
   PRIORITIES AND MAKE
   SOME CHANGES

C) GET A NEW JOB

DREAM BIG, PLAN SMALL

The Good, the Bad, the Gross.

The job you didn't get, the failed exam,
the questionable wrap you bought
from the falafel cart down the road;
there's a lesson to be learnt from every
experience. You might not realize
it at the time, but you'll be surprised
when you look back. It's all relevant.

Vagus, Baby!

The vagus nerve runs down your torso, connecting your brain and your gut. When we get that sinking feeling in the pit of our stomach, it's our brain communicating that something isn't quite right. The next time your tummy starts rumbling, unless it's hunger or last night's takeaway, consider what could be subconsciously bothering you.

There's science behind following your gut. If you don't trust your intuition, you might end up with a whole lot of shoulda, woulda, coulda's.

Eat the Pizza.

Don't punish yourself for doing what
makes you happy. Pizza is delicious,
you need not deprive yourself of such
a wonderful thing. The same goes for
anything else that might tickle your fancy.

If it means joining the circus, becoming
a dog surfing instructor, or a professional
fortune cookie writer, pursue it.

Make Up Your Own Mind.

Ask for people's advice, but don't feel you need to take it. Their guidance is based on their own experiences and circumstances; they can't speak for yours.

Listen to their opinion, process the information and then ignore it and do exactly the opposite if you want.

Be More 'Child'.

WHY?
Because children are curious about everything.

WHY?
Because they have great imaginations and no inhibitions.

WHY?
Because they're oblivious to being ridiculed.

WHY?
Because they haven't experienced embarrassment.

WHY?
Because these are things we learn as we grow older.

WHY?
Because we start to notice the shitty parts of society.

WHY?
Because we stop seeing the magic.

WHY?
Because we grow up.

WHY?
Because we have to eventually.

WHY?
Because life makes us.

WHY?
It just does.

BUT, WHY?
It just fucking does.

Don't Hand in Your Notice Until You Have a Backup Plan.

The novelty of quitting your job will wear off very quickly. Your boss has bigger issues on their mind and your office will move on faster than the time it takes to publish your Glassdoor review. The next thing you know, you're unemployed for eight months and none of your jeans fit.

No matter how much you despise your office and detest everyone and everything within it, ride it out until you have another viable option.

Having said that ...

No Job Is Worth Your Sanity.

The likelihood is that you will have more jobs you'll hate than jobs you'll enjoy. It's character building. However, when you start losing sleep and your health begins to suffer, maybe you should consider a Plan B.

A Moment of Seriousness.

I spent my twenties doing so much, but equally, not much at all. By 21 I'd achieved what I'd set out to do: completed the degree, got the awards, secured my dream job. But after some time, I arrived at the harsh reality that it didn't fulfil me. I'd been following the wrong path. Just like that, I had no focus, lots of energy but nowhere to invest it. Endless hours were spent searching for jobs that were of no real interest, mindlessly filling in applications only to be told that my CV 'didn't follow a linear path.' There was a point where I would've agreed to any job, just because it was a job. It was a decade filled with confusion and anxiety about where I was going in life.

I know what it's like being asked what you do for a living and having to reply, 'I'm unemployed'. Or being asked, 'What d'you want to do?', and genuinely not having an answer. Those experiences led me to this book. Now in my thirties, I still don't know what I'm doing with my life, and maybe I never will, but what I do know is life's too short to stay in a job you hate, and things are better as lists:

**People do want to help you, but you
must be willing to be vulnerable.**

Self-doubt gets you nowhere.

There's no such thing as the perfect job.

Don't forget to have fun.

People will always ask for a free signed copy.

Kind Regards & Best Wishes.

To all the contributors: Adam Day-Lewin, Cassandra Stavrou MBE, Chrissie Rucker OBE, Clare Smyth MBE, Derren Brown, Kathleen Saxton, Luke Hyams, Mr Bingo, Rory Sutherland, Sam Conniff, Sarah Doukas, Toni Petersson, Tory Burch and Vikki Ross – it wouldn't have been the same without you.

A huge thanks goes to the people I had to go through to get to them: Helena, Anna, Grace, Rose, Alexia, Frances and 'Brookie Cookie', Nelly, Peter, Ashlie and Michael.

To Pirate Sam, someone I've been unashamedly annoying since 2012: I'm eternally grateful for your encouragement (and connections). To my university tutor, Lynette, whose love of negative space and hate for 'thinking outside the box' inspired many pages. To Issy for never ignoring a WhatsApp request and muchas gracias to Milan who played a vital role during the early stages.

A generous dollop of gratitude goes to Elen, an editorial empress. Big thanks to Holly, who has made this process so smooth sailing. To Eleni, Katherine, Sara and the rest of the team at Laurence King, it's been a pleasure working with you all. Simon Landrein: thanks for bringing the words to life in the most perfectly peculiar way.

Lastly, to all the assholes I've had the displeasure of working with: thank you. Without you, this book wouldn't have been possible.

CARINA

carinamaggar.com

First published in Great Britain in 2022
by Laurence King, an imprint
of The Orion Publishing Group Ltd.,
Carmelite House, 50 Victoria Embankment,
London EC4Y 0DZ

An Hachette UK Company

10 9 8 7 6 5 4 3

Illustrations © 2022 Simon Landrein
Text © 2022 Carina Maggar

A CIP catalogue record for this book is
available from the British Library.

ISBN 978 08578 2 902 3

Commissioning editor: Elen Jones
Senior editor: Sara Goldsmith
Design: Eleni Caulcott

Origination by DL Imaging, London
Printed in China by C&C Offset Printing Co. Ltd.

THE LEGAL STUFF

MIX
Paper | Supporting
responsible forestry
FSC® C104740

www.laurenceking.com
www.orionbooks.co.uk